Owl Mandala Illustrations Coloring Book

Beautiful Renditions of Owl Mandalas Coloring Book

Owl Mandala

By : Gala Publication

Published By :

Gala Publication
© Copyright 2015 – Gala Publication

ISBN-13: **978-1522722205**
ISBN-10: **1522722203**

Design 1

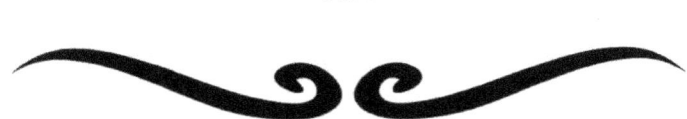

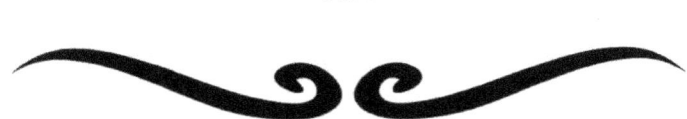

4

Design 2

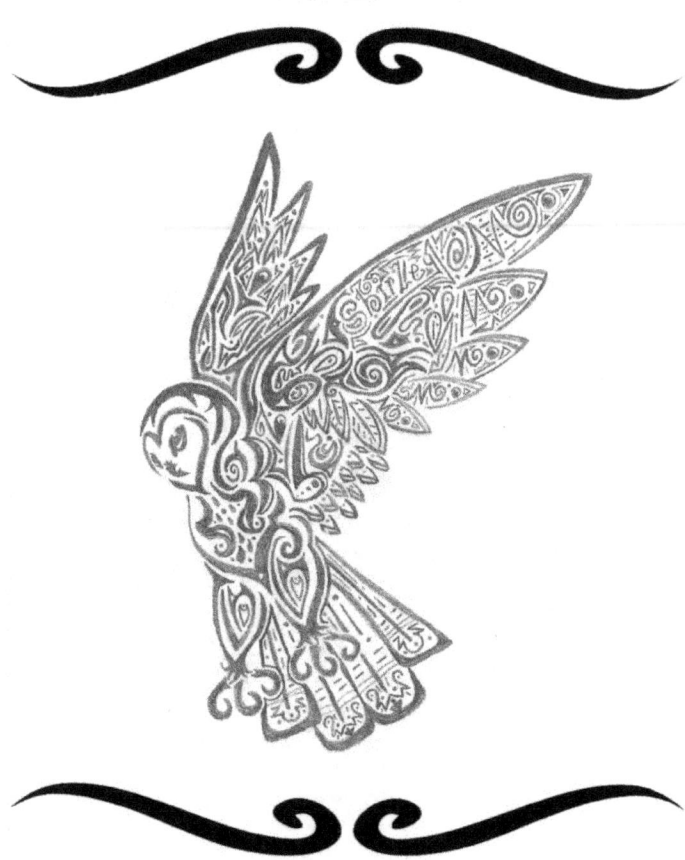

Design 3

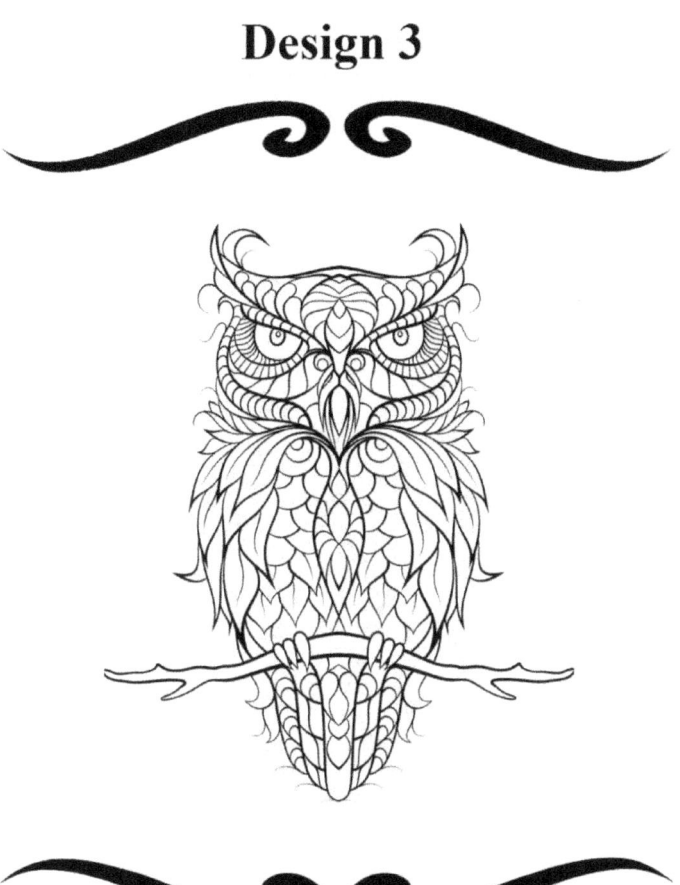

Design 4

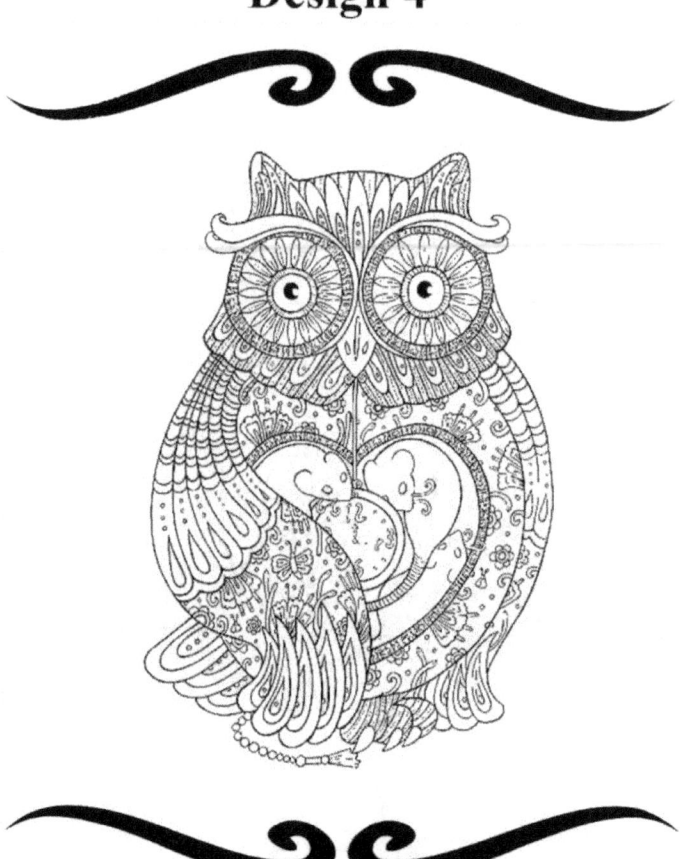

Design 5

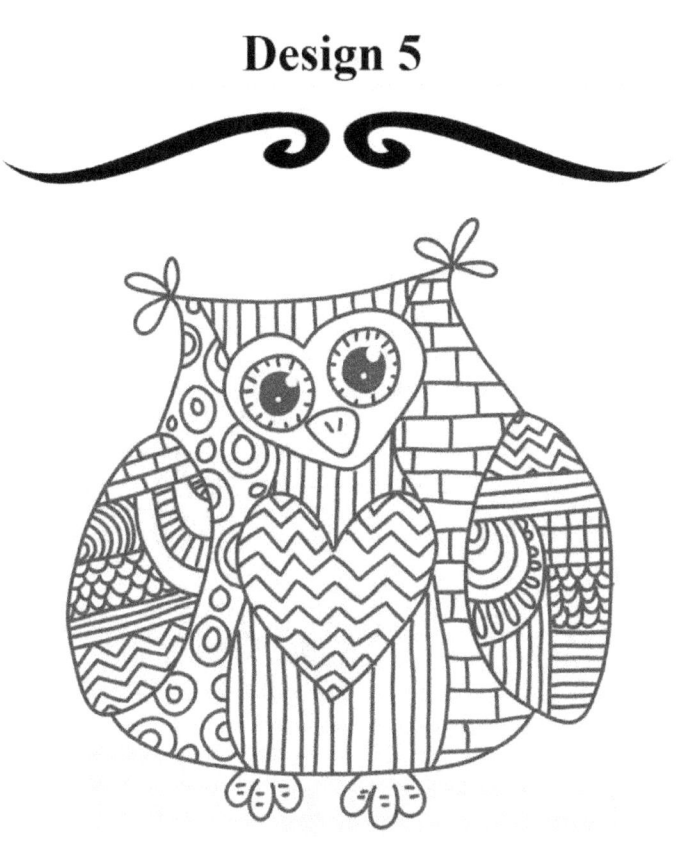

Design 6

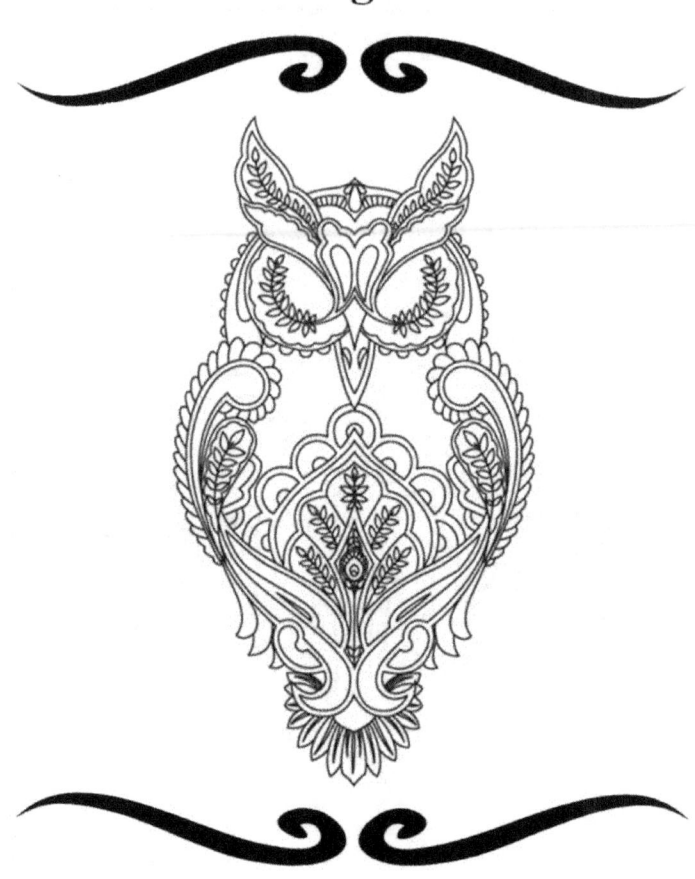

Design 7

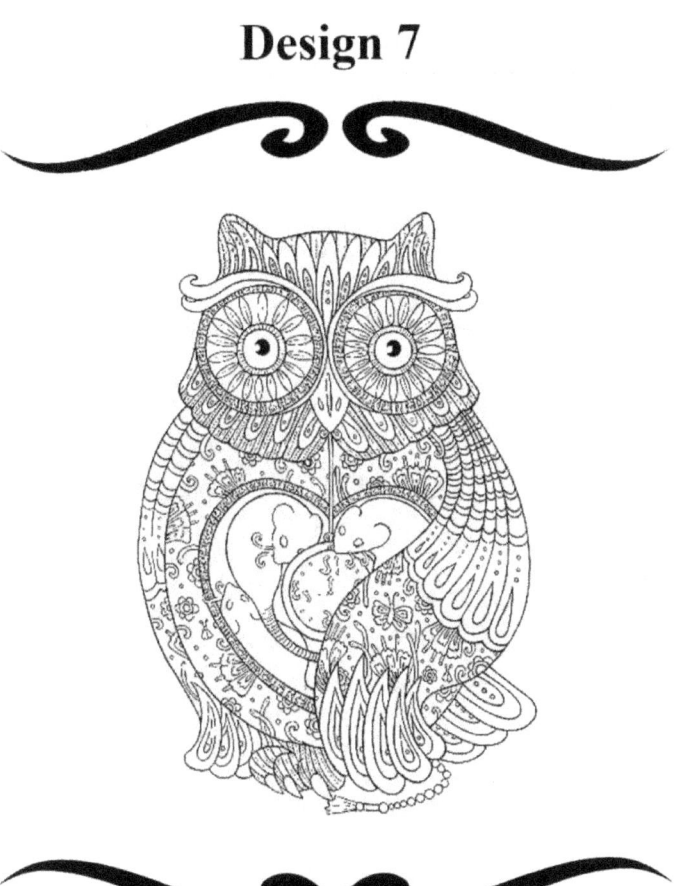

Design 8

Design 9

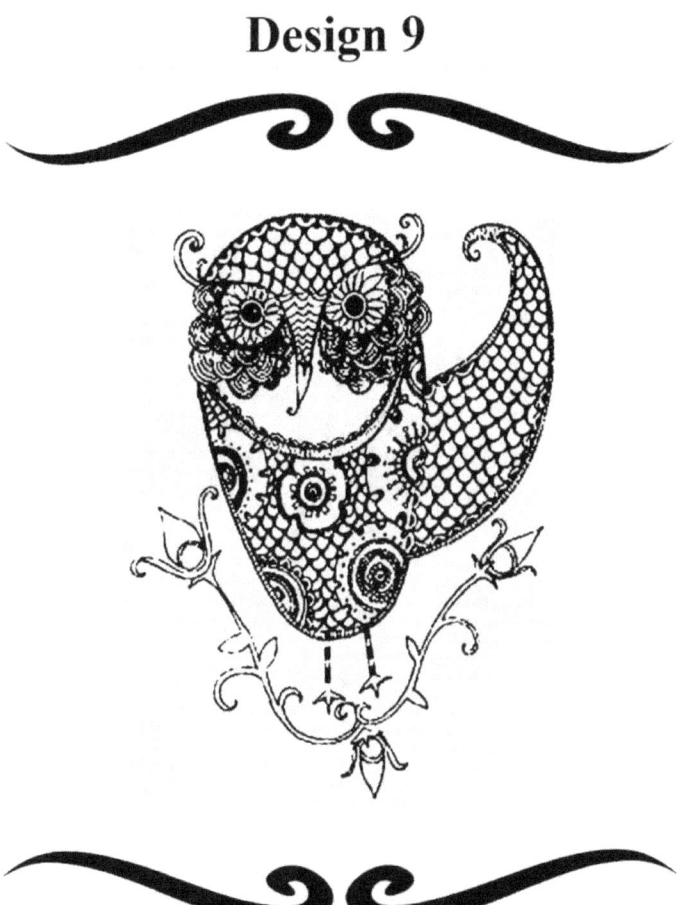

Design 10

Design 11

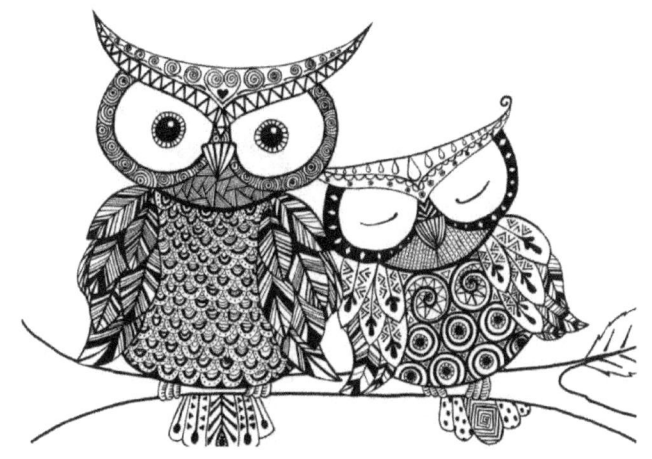

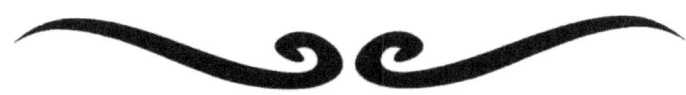

Design 12

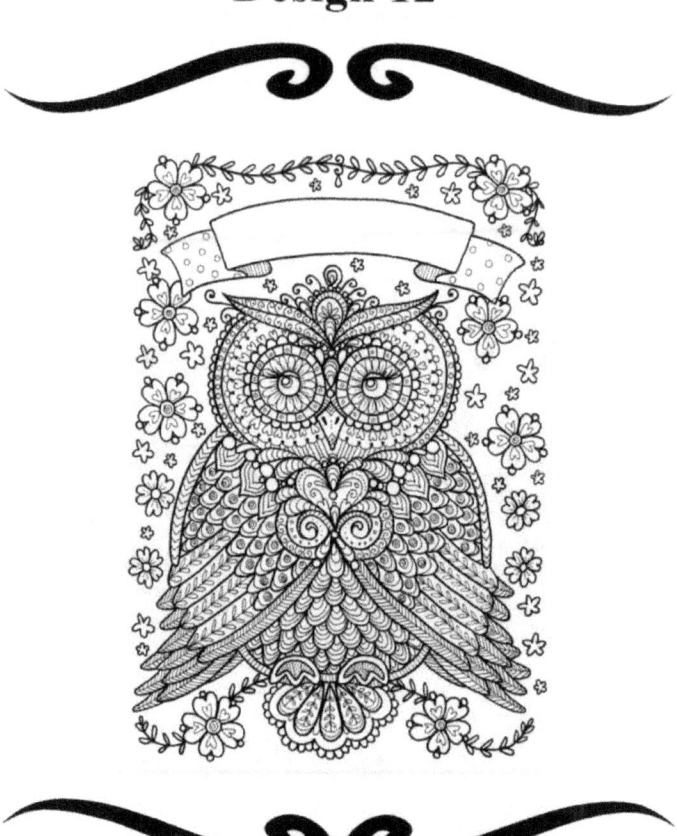

Design 13

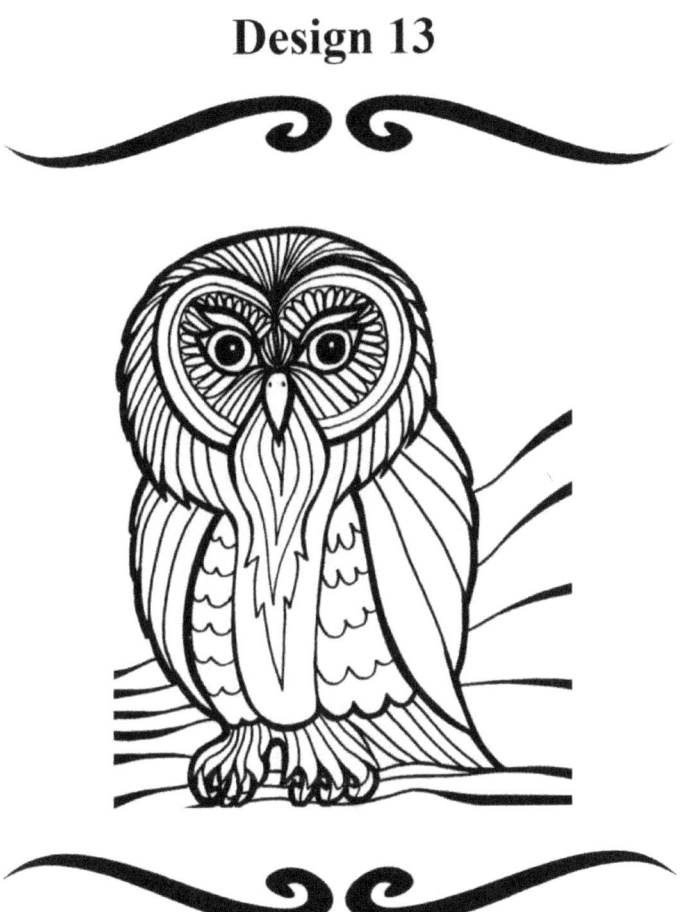

Design 14

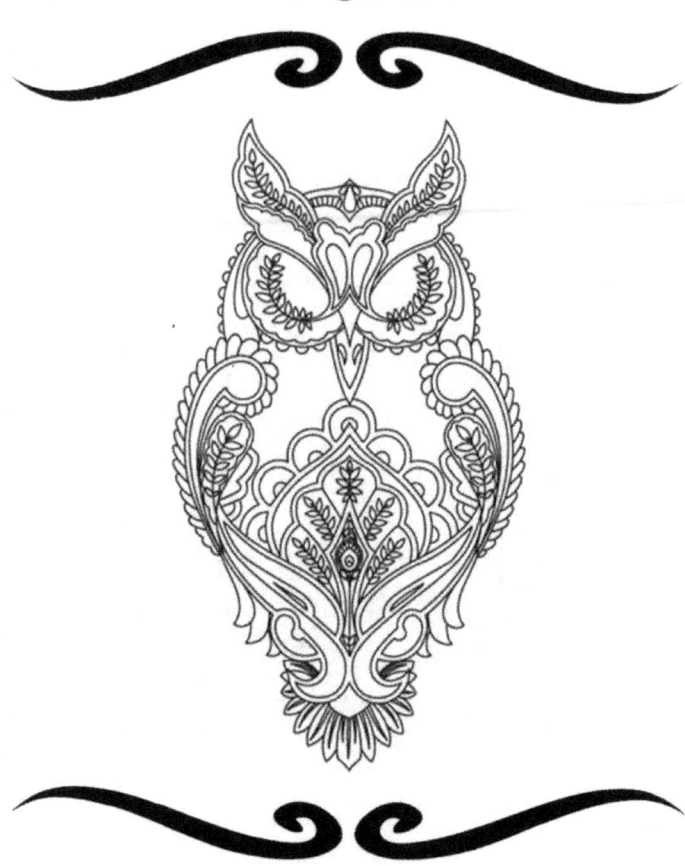

Design 15

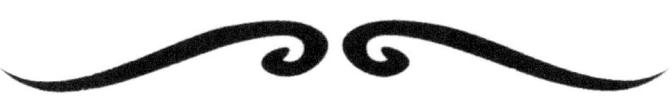

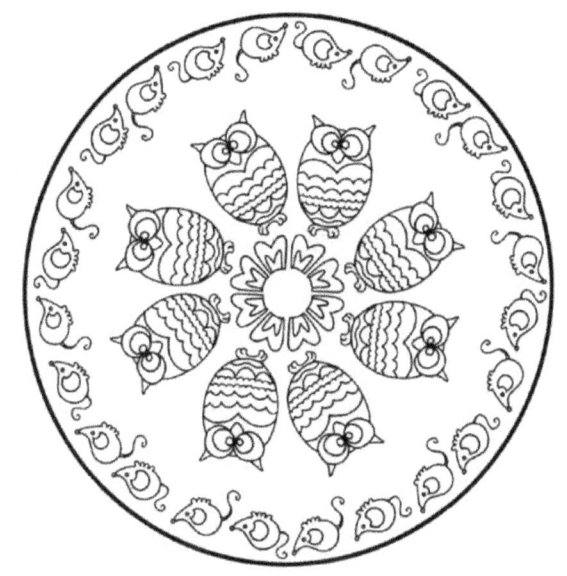

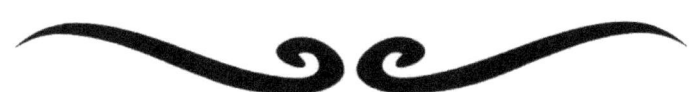

Design 16

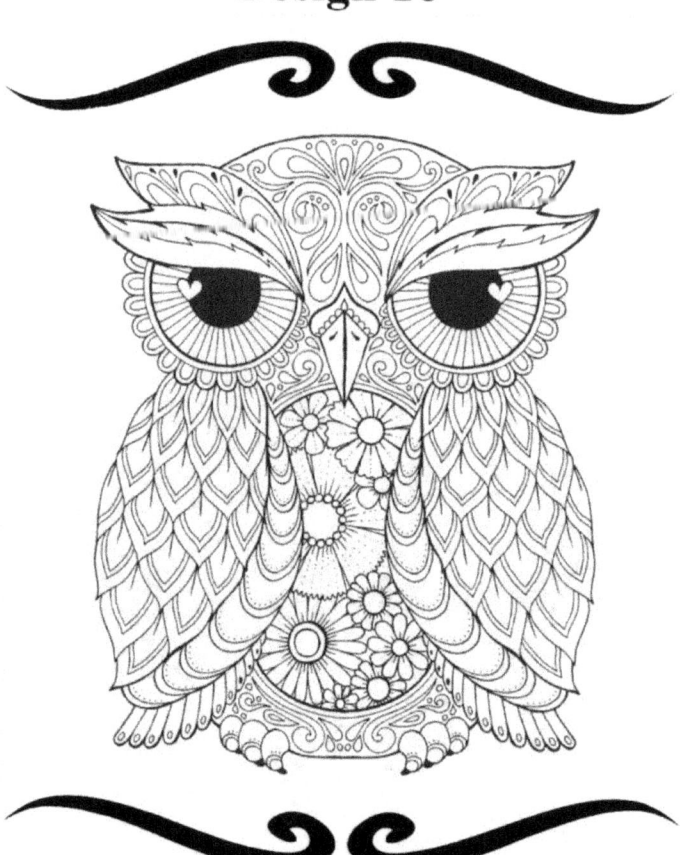

Design 17

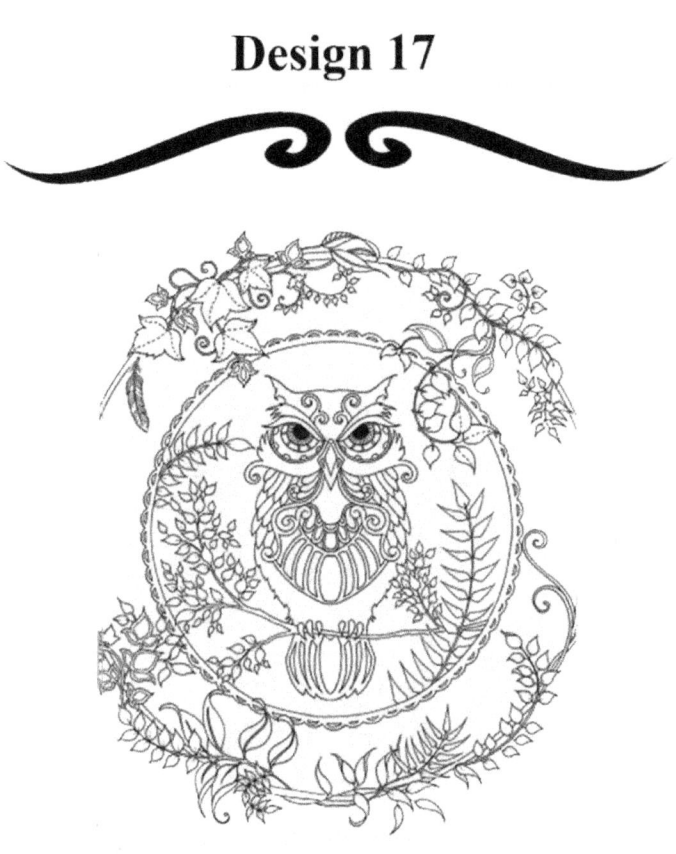

Design 18

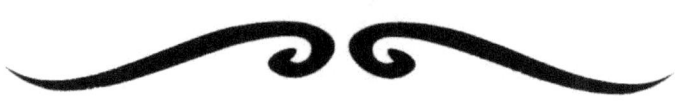

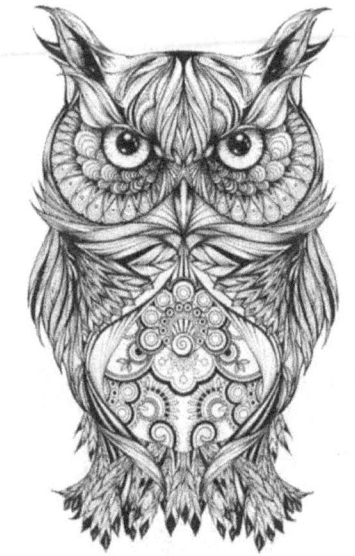

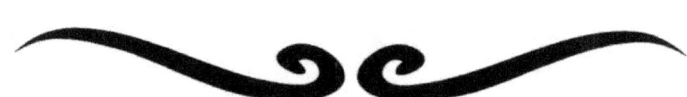

Design 19

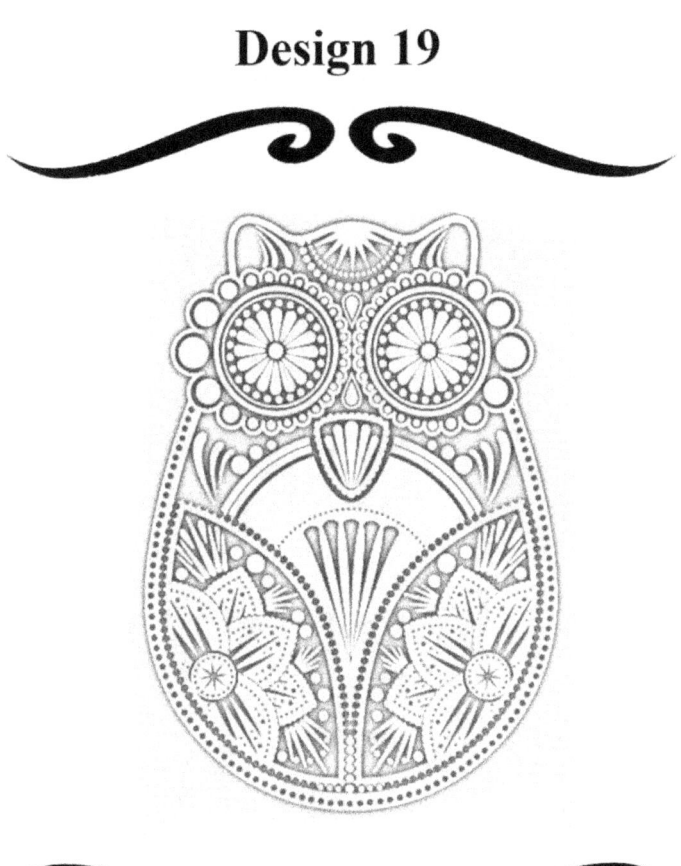

Design 20

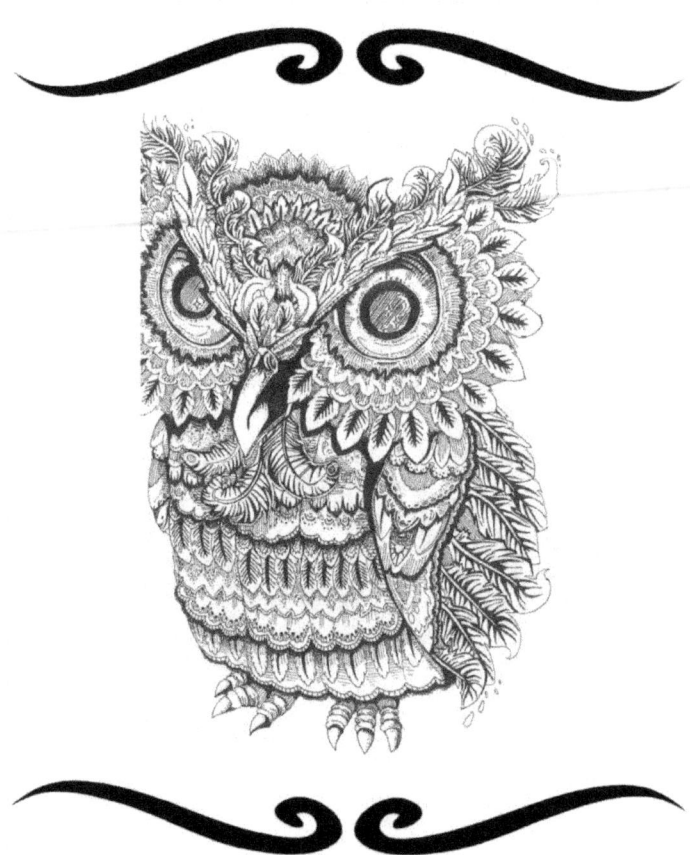

Design 21

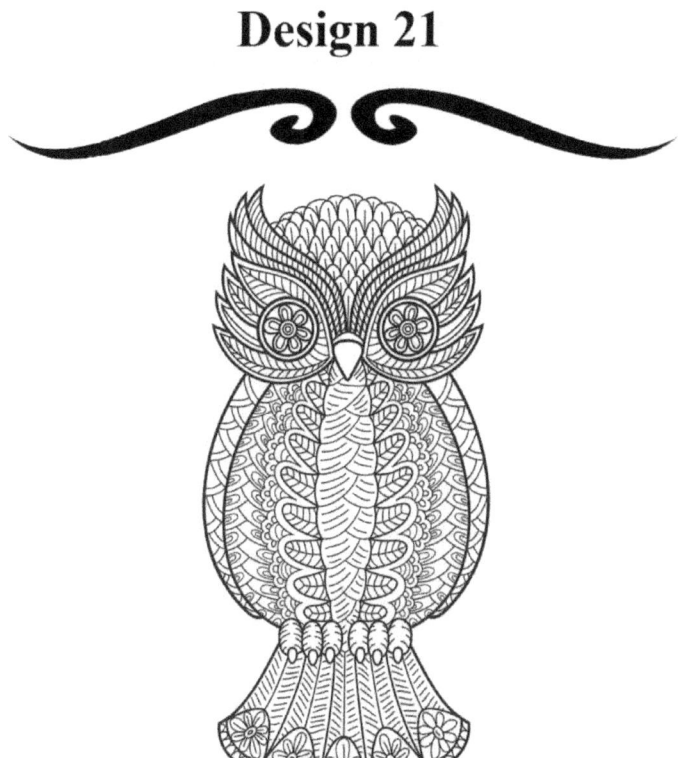

24

Design 22

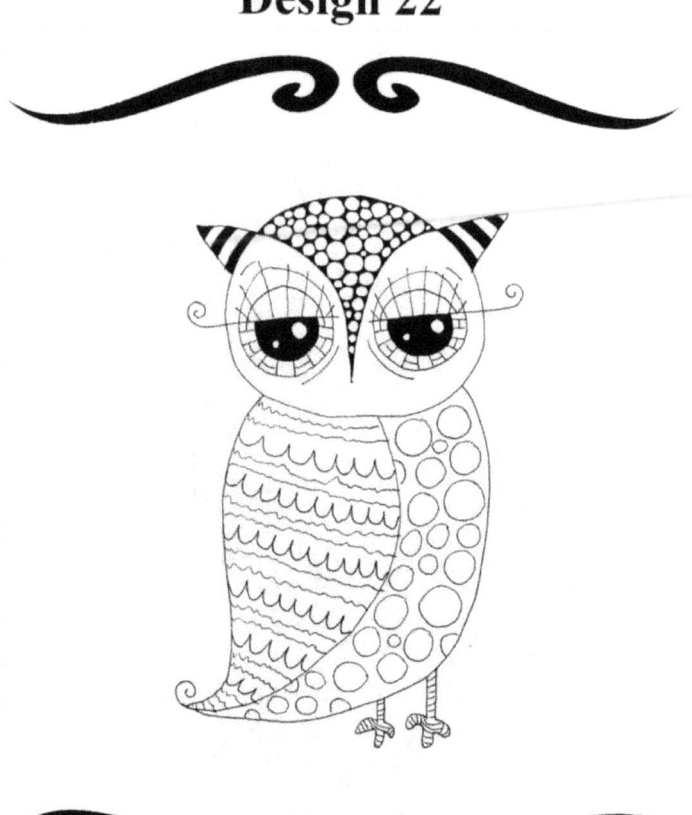

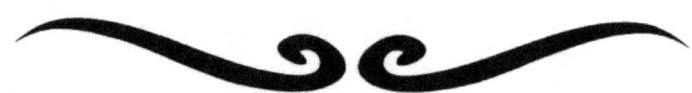

Design 23

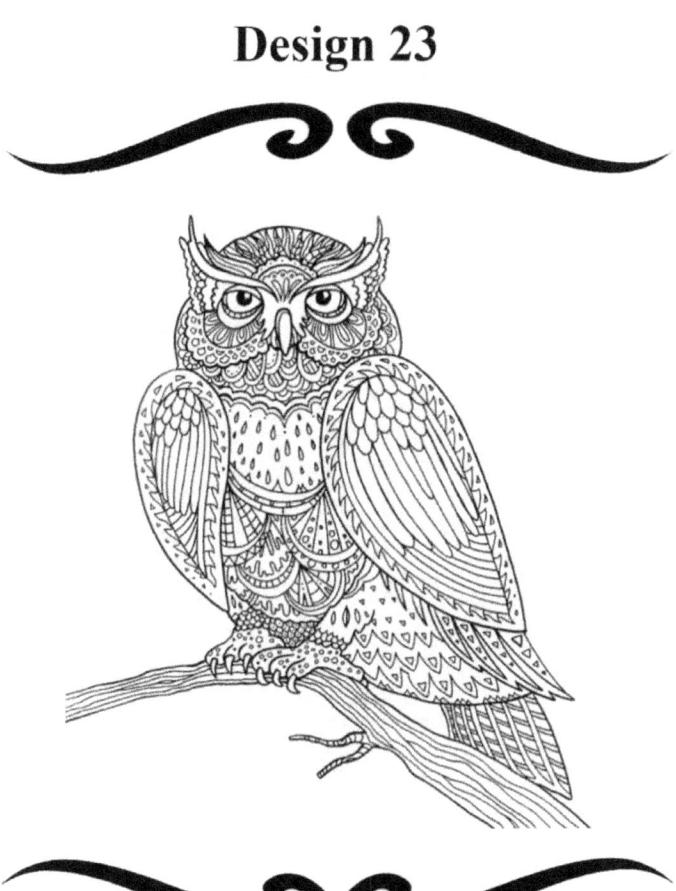

Design 24

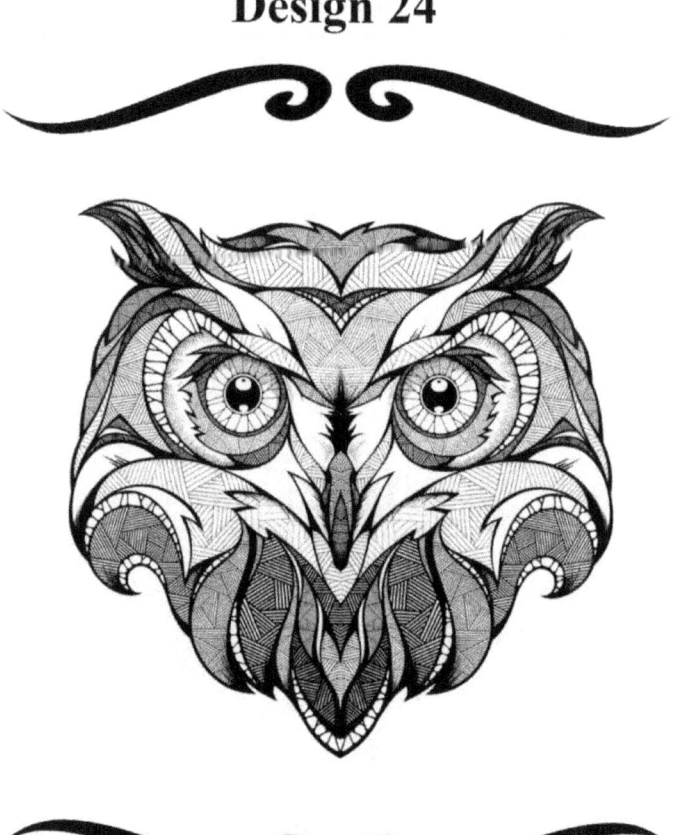

Design 25

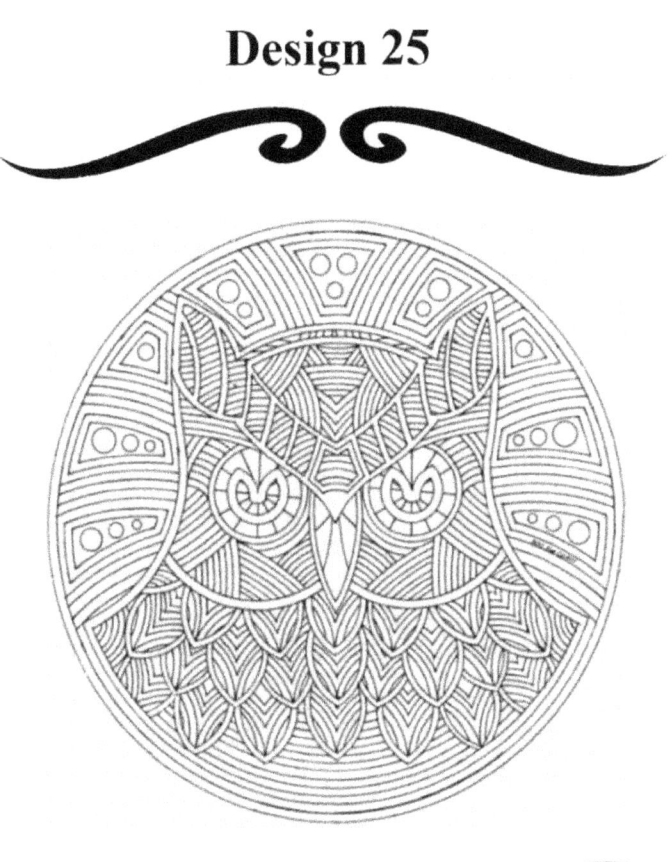

www.ingramcontent.com/pod-product-compliance
Lightning Source LLC
Chambersburg PA
CBHW071603170526
45166CB00004B/1773